ORIGIN OF ANARCHISM

BY

C. L. JAMES

CHICAGO, ILL.
A. ISAAK, PUBLISHER
1902

This copy of the
Origin of Anarchism
was the property of
Henry Bool of
Ithica N.Y. He gave it
to Joseph A. Labadie.
according to the accont of
the list of things made
out by Jo and Mrs. Labadie
to be found in the
"Labadie Collection"
Box.

Agnes Inglis.

ORIGIN OF ANARCHISM.

Anarchism, it can hardly be necessary to say, is not a conspiracy for the assassination of kings and such-like. It is not an armed movement of the proletariat or of a part of them. It is not a secret organization. Notions of its nature such as people of information have abandoned to journalists, journalists to politicians, and politicians to Mr. Roosevelt, require no further refutation. Anarchism, whatever it may give rise to, can be described as a theory only. The *thesis* of Anarchism is that men govern men by deceiving them—a view never very unfamiliar to statesmen like Machiavelli, but which evidently assumes a somewhat novel complexion when preached to the people who are governed. Anarchism is a system, a doctrine, a religion if you will, for it has been abundantly proved to inspire all the moral earnestness and to comprehend all the transcendental range of view which characterizes religions properly so called. I have undertaken here only to treat of this opinion historically, not to defend it; tho I am ready enough upon occasion to do that.

For the origin of the opinion in its modern phase, we must look to the peculiar conditions of England after the memorable year 1688. The reigning dynasty rested its claims on the result of a popular revolution. It was compelled, therefore, by the logic of its position, to favor those very principles which folks in office generally discourage. The equality of mankind, the popular origin of authority, the responsibility of rulers to the multitude, the right of the people to abolish mischievous institutions and cashier sovereigns, were the title-deeds of Kings William III, George I, and George II. Accordingly, tho the majority of clergymen, lawyers, soldiers, sailors, country gentlemen and country voters, were friends to the royal prerogative; yet bishoprics, deaneries, judgeships, brigades, admiralties, peerages, and magistracies, were almost entirely reserved for its enemies. Thus the Tory party, tho very strong, was an opposition party. While the Whigs proved that government had no excuse for existing unless it served the public good, the Tories, during more than sixty years, were proving, quite as successfully, that the most popular government which had ever existed did not serve the public good. For Whiggism, in power, took as kindly as Toryism to the standing army, martial law, the moneyed interest, monopolies, religious discriminations, pensions, sinecures, rotten boroughs; nor did Toryism, out of power, find it any harder than had Whiggism found it to expose abuses. The catch-word of Liberty, suited either faction equally well. Macaulay, who has traced these tendencies in his usual felicitous manner, remarks that what happened at the first presentation of Addison's "Cato" was, in miniature, the history of two generations. A drama whose whole merit consists in some fine rhetorical passages about hating tyrants and dying for liberty, was produced at a time of political excitement. Both parties crowded into the theater. Each affected to consider itself complimented, and its opponents attacked, in every scene. The curtain fell amidst unanimous applause. The Whigs of the Kit Cat embraced the author, and assured him he had rendered an inestimable service to liberty. The Tory secretary of State presented to the chief actor a purse, for defending the cause of liberty so well.

Thus fiercely assailed on two opposite sides, government, for the first time, began to appear mortal in the eyes of a few discerning men. Burke's "Vindication of Natural Society" (1760) is, indeed, represented as a satire; but it was too good for the purpose. There is no reason to doubt that it represented suspicions which had actually arisen in the author's capacious and restless mind. Two thoughts operated as the centrifugal and centripetal forces of all Burke's philosophy—that human nature is indefinitely improvable, and that precedent is the logic of authority. Put in the form of major and minor, they should evidently produce the conclusions of Anarchism. Anarchists still refer to the "Vindication" for proofs, no less unanswerable because offered in a way which discouraged serious reply, that protection, such as government offers against foreign and domestic violence, is not a source of safety but of danger. *From that time, neither England nor America has ever been without Anarchistic writers.* Within twelve years, the Junius letters were holding up authority as the worst of evils. "In vain you tell me," cried Burke, "that artificial government is good and that I fall out only with the abuse. The thing! the thing itself is the abuse!" In the first letter of Junius, he strikes the very key-note of his composition, thus. "It is not the disorder, but the physician; it is the pernicious hand of government alone which can make a whole people desperate." The radical thought is the same. The protection afforded by police, armies, navies, is nugatory. It creates greater evils than it averts—chief among them the habit of relying upon authority, not on native force of will, which alone saves any people from slavery or extinction.

Burke retired from public affairs in 1794, and died in 1797. In the most terrible year of the French Revolution, 1793, while he was still at head of the dominant and reactionary party in England, Godwin's "Political Justice" gave to English Anarchism a form which could neither be overlooked nor disregarded as merely ironical. Godwin did not possess Burke's or Junius' denunciatory power; but his coldly logical nature grasped more firmly than either of them the idea which they had in common. "Government, *in its very nature*," he wrote, "counteracts the improvement of original mind." This "improvement of original mind," was Godwin's *summum bonum*. He could not sacrifice it to "the logic of nations," like Burke, or imagine it reconciled with its natural antagonist, like other precursors of Anarchism. Those who have heard of his "Political Justice" only as a Communistic book, may need to be informed that, after encountering Malthus, he softened a little his Socialism, but never his plea for absolute personal independence.

Godwin's son-in-law, Shelley, and Shelley's most intimate friend, Byron, enshrined the new wisdom in immortal verse. It seems incredible anyone should be unaware of Shelley's Anarchism, which his earliest poem of any note put in such unmistakable words as these:

"The man
Of virtuous soul commands not, nor obeys:
Power, like a desolating pestilence,
Pollutes whate'er it touches, and obedience

Bane of all genius, virtue, freedom, truth,
Makes slaves of men, and, of the human frame,
A mechanized automaton."

It is harder to demonstrate Byron's Anarchism by citations; for the prevailing spirit of his works is what we chiefly infer it from. Still bolder might seem the attempt to offer anything like an adequate theory of Byronism, even now. This, however, is not likely to be disputed, that all Philistia regarded Byron as the embodied spirit of what Philistines call chaos and destruction. He appeared to England what Voltaire had seemed to France, a man of the highest and most versatile genius, who did not, like Hume or Gibbon, Godwin or Paine, assail existing ideas of morality, religion, and government, argumentatively, but who evidently had no respect for them, and whose equal power of sublimity and of humor was never shown so characteristically as when making them odious or ridiculous. A thousand times it was prophesied that his influence would be ephemeral. But this prediction, we are now justified in saying, has proved erroneous. The fad of imitating Byron soon died out, of course; but neither to critics nor mere readers, English or foreigners, is Byron's place in English literature much less important now than it was eighty years ago. What is the secret of his continued strength? It is not surely, his appeal to personal spmpathy. That has long been considered his weakest point. It is not the novelty of his brilliant description; for the novelty has faded, and the descriptions can hardly profess to be better than those of Scott or Wordsworth. It is not the originality of his verse, for even in his own time critics could see that there was none. Nor is it to be denied that Byron was no dramatist or master of human nature; not one of those who live in song, like Keats, by the exquisite completeness of their art; not one of those who, like Cowper, have imbued the humblest natural objects with human sympathy. Byron remains, as he always was, the prophet of individual life. His influence owes its permanence to nothing else so much as this, that "improvement of original mind" is the spirit of an age which rather began than ended with his writings. It would be quite unnecessary to cite passages showing his contempt for kings, priests, nobles, institutions, maxims, conventionalities; but it is worth while to remark at this point that his radicalism stopped at no wayside inn like democracy.

"I'd have mankind be free
As much from mobs as kings—from you as me."

Friends of Byron, Shelley, or each other, Leigh Hunt, Charles Lamb, Landor, who fully represented the spirit of these great men, carried it on to the time when such more modern English literateurs as Swinburne and William Morris were ready to enter the arena.

In America, immediately after Junius, Anarchistic doctrine had made its début with the early writings of Jefferson and the political works of Thomas Paine. A certain resemblance may be traced between the lives as well as the sentiments of these famous men, who, it may be remembered, were close friends. Both experienced the growing doubt whether government in any form were not a mere device of the powerful and cunning to enslave the weak and simple. Both took part in the American revolution, and afterwards in the French. Both were drawn into the vortex of practical politics. But Jefferson's cool head and worldly talents were adapted to other things than Paine's fiery zeal against injustice and oppression. In Jefferson's early writings he repeatedly observes that it is possible to imagine a community without a government, and that there even are such communities. He expresses great doubt whether this primitive form of association be not the best; and says it admits of no comparison with the graded monarchies of Europe. He added to the Constitution the first few amendments, which are its best part, and which owe their merit to this, that they are limitations of those powers else likely to be exercised by the State or federal government. He became the successful candidate of the party opposed to centralization, and to increase of legislative or executive authority. But, as president, he took a step, in the Louisiana Purchase, which introduced into our institutions the pernicious doctrine of indefinite powers lodged in the chief magistrate for use on special occasions, and set an example for those piratical crimes of annexation, whose atrocious climax we now see in the Philippine Islands.

Paine, in his earliest acknowledged political treatise, strikes the chord of his entire strain by protesting against confusion of government with society. "Society in every state is a blessing; but government, even in its best state, is but a necessary evil, in its worst state an intolerable one; for when we suffer or are exposed to the same miseries by a government which we might expect in a country without a government our calamity is heightened by the reflection that we furnish the means by which we suffer." It is difficult to believe that his view of government was more favorable after his experience in the French National Convention than before.

During the generation following the death of Jefferson (1826), there were many American Anarchists, tho most of them are rather obscure, and the Anarchism of others has been artificially kept out of sight. First in literary celebrity stand Emerson and Thoreau, who require a place by themselves. The sons of William Lloyd Garrison tell us, not only that he was an Anarchist, which numerous passages in his own correspondence prove, but that his friends found some difficulty about deterring him from merging his abolitionism in a crusade against all positive institutions. Colonel Greene's book, "The Blazing Star," little known, I believe, except among American Anarchists, puts in rather fanciful form the exact doctrine of Godwin and the historic-transcendental school which followed Hegel. The Blazing Star is the idea of human perfectibility. It is "the improvement of original mind." Like Godwin, like Shelley, like Byron, like Emerson, like Thoreau, like Condorcet, like Proudhon, like Herbert Spencer in his best essays, such as that on "Over Legislation," Greene perceives that authority, in every form, "counteracts the improvement of original mind." It is the antithesis of the Blazing Star. It is the chilling fog of precedent; that is, of old time ignorance and barbarism. The doctrine, historically vindicated with considerable ability, is not this meaningless cant that if men were perfect they would be fit for absolute individual freedom: it is that every step towards the perfection of humanity begins with some assertion of absolute individual freedom.

As regards the economic aspects of Anarchism, the first place among Americans belongs to Josiah Warren (grandson of that Warren who fell at Bunker Hill). He shared in the innumerable experiments of the Fourieristic type which at one time were tried in America, and, as he tells us, became wearied, without being discouraged, by their uniform failure.

At last a light broke in upon him. The fault of existing economic and social arrangements is not too much competition, as the Communists were in the habit of saying, but too little. In a world of landlords, charters, monopolies, and legislative restrictions, free competition is nowhere to be found, because absolute individual freedom is nowhere to be found. The plan, adopted by all Communistic settlements, of putting the members under restraints more severe than those of ordinary society, may succeed when there are few enough of them to be united by a dogmatical religion like that of the Shakers, but not otherwise. Therefore, it is wrong in principle. The way to reach the golden east is to sail west across the open sea. Free competition must reduce prices to the cost of production; which would be practical Communism. This American anticipation of Marx and Proudhon, from whom it does not appear the author learned anything, attracted the very respectful notice of John Stuart Mill.

It is an open secret that our great lawyer, Charles O'Connor, was an Anarchist, and that is why he declined to be a candidate for president of the United States.

Thus purely indigenous English and American Anarchism is much earlier than the French, German, or Russian kind. It is, therefore, quite a mistake to regard Anarchism as a peculiarity of the "foreigners," against whom there is so much foolish prejudice. Anarchism is the child of our own institutions; and they have got to rear it.

There was, indeed, one French Revolutionist, the famous mathematician and *philosophe* Condorcet, who really was an Anarchist, as early as 1794, when he died, leaving his views embodied in a posthumous work, "The Progress of the Human Mind"; upon which his fame principally rests. Nothing is more inspiring than the optimistic tone of this book, written in daily expectation of the guillotine, by one who had seen all his plans frustrated, his party proscribed, and the great movement which drew him from his peaceful studies into the heated arena of politics disgraced by the atrocities of the Great Committee. The perfectibility of humanity is the central idea. Condorcet was not, like Godwin, Shelley, Byron, Emerson, or Thoreau, a Transcendental pantheist; at any rate the tone of his reasoning was altogether Positive and materialistic. Man, originally only an animal, distinguished by limited powers but unlimited ferocity and rapacity, has proved indefinitely improvable because his strength is all in his intellect, which, unlike any bodily gift, can be cultivated and developed *ad infinitum*. The original form of social organization, Condorcet perceived, was not the family, but the nomadic horde. With the domesticating of animals, property and marriage came in. These two stages of human progress, and the next, that of primitive agriculture, are known only by inference. But for the rest we have records. Subsequent progress is divided into six stages, of which one is assigned to Grecian civilization, one to Roman, a third to the Middle Ages preceding the Crusades. The fourth extends to the invention of printing; the fifth to the rise of inductive philosophy with Descartes; the sixth to the French Revolution. Condorcet prophecies that the same causes which have so far determined the progress of the human mind, will introduce, with the next stage, equality of nations and of individuals. It will be recognized that tho nations are not equal in material power, they are in respect to the value of those functions by which they severally contribute to human advance; and the same is true of the individuals composing each community. To tyrannize over a weaker person, or nation, is, accordingly, to cripple humanity, and thus to injure the oppressor. The perfectibility of humanity being thus recognized, progress, hitherto spasmodic and frequently impeded by contention, will become uniform and rapid. There are reasons for believing that these sanguine predictions were not visionary. THE REVOLUTION, as radicals call it, that great Revolution, which began in England with the accession of George III, and in which the revolutions of America and France are only incidents, originated, as we have seen, in the realization by a few, that humanity is indefinitely improvable, and that Law, our inheritance from ignorant barbarous ancestors, is the standing obstacle to "the improvement of original mind." That Revolution, however it may be protracted, is not likely to end until recognition of its fundamental principles becomes general.

Condorcet, however, left no party. He died just in time to escape the guillotine. The French Revolution was not at all an Anarchistic event; tho some ignoramuses suppose it was. Its watchword was always *la loi*, from the first contests of Louis XV with his parliament to the overthrow of the Great Committee's tyranny by a simple vote of the Convention. The number of prominent Revolutionists who were lawyers is among the most significant peculiarities of the movement. Anarchy reigned during the Revolution only at those periods when the imbecility and senility of law had made its disregard a necessity too palpable for denial. The French Revolution contributed to Anarchistic sentiment, only thru the frequency of these occurrences. Its legislative absurdities—that people must *thou* and *thee* each other, wear liberty-caps and working clothes, etc., etc.—were Red Republican affectations, with which Anarchists have nothing to do.

It was not until about 1848, that Proudhon formulated Continental Anarchism.

Meanwhile the soil had been prepared in other ways. The metaphysical doctrine that man has a "natural right" to do whatever does not "invade" the "equal rights" of others, and that "restraint" on the conduct of individuals should be limited to preventing such "invasion," has often been confounded with Anarchism, but is really very different. Like all metaphysics, it states a principle so wide as to involve what Kant would have called an "~~antimony~~" which nullifies it in practise. Who is to decide what does invade the equal rights of others, and therefore require restraint, if not the government or dominant power? Jefferson's coquettings with the Scarlet Lady, who hails from Rome, and whose name is Authority, probably give him a better claim than has anyone else to be presumed the father of this bastard Anarchism, on which the title of Individualism has been fixed. It wore, at any rate, for pinafore, the French Declaration of the Rights of Man, which is very like a piece of his work. But its most successful dry-nurse has, beyond a doubt, been Herbert Spencer. Now Anarchism, as we have traced it, is not metaphysical but positive. It affirms, as Carlyle would say, not the speculative Rights, but the practical Mights of Man. It affirms, not barely that men ought not be governed by their fellow men, but that they cannot be so governed without a certain compliance on their own part; and that such compliance depends upon their being previously deluded. The proof of this is inductive. It consists in proof that whenever men chose, they have been able to get rid of authority and restraint, and to introduce Anarchy into certain important departments of human action, with results invariably favorable to what they regarded as their best interests. During the interval between 1760 and 1848, this had to a great extent been done. Jefferson and Franklin had popularized the idea of Anarchy in religion. Adam Smith had brought into favor Anarchy in trade. The later economists, Bentham probably in particular, had so enlarged upon the mischief which legislation and politics do to business, that many bourgeois writers, it is well known, have, following them, come as near to Anarchism as possible, and only apparently shrunk from endangering the sanctity of "property" —out of fear for their personal interests, or perhaps lest they should quarrel with the dominant class. Herbert Spencer, as usual, is the great example. During the same period, Saint Simon had grasped the notion of social evolution, and predicted that thru the same economic series of causes and effects which made the bourgeois system supplant the feudal, ownership of industrial establishment by the operatives would displace it. The German Transcendentalists, carrying further the principle of the Reformation, which affirmed the supremacy of subjective *faith* over objective *law*, had traced the soul's orbit to itself, and proclaimed the emancipation of individual man. Carlyle, Emerson, and Thoreau, had popularized their work for English readers. The writings of all three are quite Anarchist text books. Here, it may be said, we have certainly reached metaphysics at last! Not, however, in such a manner as to make it the basis of Anarchistic theory or practise.

The three principal authors of Anarchistic movements on the Continent, were Proudhon, Marx, and Bakunin. All three began as representatives of the Hegelian Left. All acknowledged indebtedness to Saint Simon, and to Adam Smith's disciples, especially Ricardo. Marx is to be classed with the other two, because his speculations were altogether Anarchistic. As one who had learned of Saint Simon, he saw in national governments military organizations foredoomed to pass away with the advance of industrialism. Whatever functions of a permanent character they possess must devolve upon trades' unions *international* in range. It was only after his movemont had absorbed Lassalle's Social

Democracy that he became too much of a politician to act with Bakunin. The fact that these eminent men disagreed so much, no more prevents their being the authors of the great Anarchistic movement than a similar unfortunate truth prevents our regarding Luther, Zwingli, Calvin, and Socinus, as the principal figures in the Reformation. They were distinguished by strong traits both of individuality and nationality. For that reason each had a work which no other could do.

Proudhon's writings are much easier to read than those of Marx; and accordingly he has received more general credit for deep thoughts, such as that property is not derived from the labor which produces it but from the primordial claim of the government, bestowed on individuals in forms like proslavery legislation, land grants, or, in our time particularly, charters of monopoly. But in truth Proudhon is important to Anarchism chiefly as an agitator. His use of the word was alone no small exploit. It was like capturing the enemy's favorite piece of artillery, and turning it against him. The bulk of Proudhon's fifty volumes consist in correspondence, tracts, pamphlets, newspaper or magazine articles, and other publications of the journalistic type. His celebrity rests chiefly on terse, epigrammatic, and paradoxical sayings, such as "Property is robbery," or "Liberty is not the daughter but the mother of order." The ideas are good enough to keep anything so well written alive and insure its circulation as missionary literature for a long time. But tho Proudhon was the most careful and deliberate of journalists, who never wrote in a hurry, still he was a journalist, often compelled to write without much previous reading, often (witness his tract on the Malthusians) writing about what he did not understand.

It hardly appears as tho any one of the three knew rightly in what his own principal strength consisted. Marx doubtless hoped to be the organizer; but this function devolved on the very apostle of Chaos, Bakunin. It is the Bakunin wing of the Anarchists, acting as individuals, rejecting direction, hitting hard, and hitting at everything instituted, who have made Anarchism a terror to tyrants and monopolists, absolutely rendered the king business extra hazardous, compelled "those who make the quarrels" to do the fighting, figured as reserve in the revolutionary movements of Spain and other countries, effected visible political results, like the victory of universal suffrage in Belgium. It is usual to say that Bakunin's ultra-destructive tendencies were the reaction against Russian despotism. I should have said that in his transcendental nihilism, so mystical and so sceptical at once, we might discern the imaginative superetherial temper of the Sclavonic race. Yet it is Russia which has produced the most unlike type of Anarchism possible—the purely religious and pacific kind. Tolstoy has no doubt made more converts to Anarchism than Bakunin; and he may make a great many more. To represent Anarchism as a corollary from Christianity is indeed to disregard the logic of facts, which teaches that from Christianity, as from other dogmatical first principles, you may draw any practical corollary you please. But Anarchism doubtless is something more than a corollary from the moral precepts of Jesus, as Tolstoy says it is. They retain their freshness, perhaps in greater purity for their never having been reduced to practise; and they have the great advantage of being perforce admitted supreme in authority by that very Antichrist whose efforts during nineteen centuries have been devoted to explaining them away. The real position of Marx among authors of recent Anarchism is that of the scientific economist. He is described by the unfriendly critic of the Encyclopedia Britannica as *facile princeps* among assailants of existing institutions, a man of vast learning, candor, and acuteness—his principal work on "Captital" as "the philosophic history of the bourgeois system." His strength is largely due to grasp of the Evolutionary philosophy, so powerfully reenforced towards the end of his life by Darwin.

In the later history of Anarchism, nothing is more remarkable than the way it has gathered strength, like some mighty river, from tributaries whose sources lie far apart. Not by eclecticism, putting together views or parts of views with little regard to consistency, but by virtue of a central position —as that attitude which covers the whole field of man's intellectual possessions in regarding "the improvement of original mind,"—does Anarchism critically filter into itself the strength both of Positive and Speculative philosophy.

The physical discoveries of such evolutionists as Lombroso and Krafft-Ebing have dealt a blow in the most vital spot of the government-superstition by disclosing the radical viciousness of those methods thru which Law affects to protect us against Crime. Law, not to mention its foolish multiplication of mere *mala prohibita*, has no other method than terrorism. Either "warning" or "removing the offender" is the sole purpose of its penalties. Even before criminology began to assume the character of a science, humane and judicious persons required to administer the law had partly found out its error. Warning does not warn. Removing one offender makes more than one. The penologists sought to substitute reformation for intimidation, and prevention for reformation. The misfortune was that their new humane plans did not succeed better than the old barbarous one. "Intimidation," one of the most distinguished among them used to say, "does not intimidate; reformation does not reform; and prevention does not prevent." To this confessed bankruptcy in the protection-against-crime corporation or trust, Crimonology brings a release. All reason, all excuse even, for continuing the insolvent business disappears upon evidence that this does more harm than good. Now Criminology teaches that neither Born nor Habitual criminals can be reformed. The former class, so far as they are dangerous, need not sensibly increase the population of insane asylums; the best chance to get rid of the latter is better social arrangements, under which whole sub-classess, pirates, for example, highwaymen, and bravoes have, thru extensive countries, disappeared. Occasional criminals can be reformed. But if a method of making this impossible be wanted, it is formulated in the words "trial and imprisonment." The bulk of professional criminals are not, in the eye of science, Habitual. They are Occasional Criminals, whom private exhortation and dismissal might have saved; but whom publicity; disgrace; bad companionship; Fagin and Bumble, Hawkshaw and Moss, acting together; have made distinguishable from fellow criminals by choice only thru certain physical stigmata. It is against the professional class of criminals that law is supposed necessary for our protection. The open secret that law principally makes them, cannot be kept a secret long. Its effect on popular reverence for law may be predicted. Cowardice is the secret of that reverence; and fear, once enlisted on the other side, will send our "civil authority" after our grandfathers' swords and pistols. In European countries, now, as during slavery times, ahead of America, the effect of criminal psychology has already been to abolish entirely most important parts of criminal law. The contempt with which criminologists treat what remains, is extreme.

Almost simultaneously with criminology, Ethnology, another outgrowth of the Evolutionary philosophy, comes to the support of Anarchistic in due season. Those views on the genesis and dissolution of institutions advanced by Sir John Lubbock and other special students of man's primitive state, are not very unlike Condorcet's; but they have the advantage of being put in a more popular form and sustained by a far wider induction. The earliest society was only a horde. King Mob is therefore the father of all sovereigns. The troop were called Wolves or Snakes, from their habits, and were proud of the title. They venerated wolves or snakes, and believed themselves descended from an animal like that whose name they bore—which animal was the Totem, or national deity. Their customs (naturally) are so absurd that they must have been abandoned long ago, but for that superstition which attributes them to the Totem's omniscient direction, and presumes that "Chaos" would instantly follow men's disregarding his instructions. From the earliest times, we can trace a divergence in their character. There is a common law, of immemorial antiquity; and there are, long before there is writing to record them, ordinances or statutes, evidently having an intelligible origin—usually something in the nature of a treaty between hordes. The common law has the advantage of being modifiable by the instincts of the people, whom it therefore always in a measure suits. It has the disadvantage of being grossly irrational. The statutes are evident attempts to better it; and often have the great advantage of repealing large portions. But they have the disadvantage of being arbitrary—commonly not being adapted to the people's habits and instincts. The true remedy for common law absurdity is the increase of general intelligence, which brings people to see that it is absurd. The great obstacle to improvement is the superstitious reverence for hereditary, that is for barbarous, institutions, which makes getting rid of them impossible until they become past all endurance. If, to illustrate, punishment, instead of being beneficial, is as noxious as every penologist has long known it is, why do penal laws continue to multiply? If a matter so private and personal as dress is as full of unsanitary and even morally mischievous absurdity as all the caricaturists have been making it out for a century, why is conformity to fashion exacted, not only by Mrs. Grundy, but even, in a great measure, by the civil authorities? Because, at the root of those common law principles enforced by the Totem's omniscience, so far as this is credited, lie two grand superstitions called in the South Sea Islands *utu* and *taboo;* of which the latter teaches that such and such actions, many quite harmless to men, are offensive to the spirits, while the other teaches that such actions must be punished, or the spirits will be angry with all of us, and—in short, "we shall have Anarchy." Knowledge of such truths can scarcely fail to excite a wholesome spirit of Protestantism against Government and Grundy.

In a very different, and, I admit, highly questionable manner, the followers of Swedenborg have brought transcendental individualism to the masses. However ill we may think of their dogmas, their influence is not to be despised. They have insured, for one thing, a wide diffusion of tendencies ripe for Anarchistic use. Scratch a Spiritualist, and you will find an Anarchist. There is still another point of view in which the movement is of value. It has been very intimately associated with the emancipation of women. This great reform was long almost confined to America; and it is from America that other nations have so far chiefly learned. But the emancipation of women, as Bakunin observed, is indispensable to the social revolution. Not only is their influence necessary to an important part of that emancipation which the men desire for themselves; but the increase of population must frustrate all attempts to prevent an upper class from rising by trampling down a lower, as long as the subjection of women makes such increase inevitable. The emancipation of women is among those fruits of the bourgeois system preluding its own passage, which were anticipated by Condorcet and Saint Simon. It began in the factories: and so far as rights of employment or property are concerned, was doubtless indebted chiefly to the convenience of the capitalists. Even here, however, it would hardly have been effected if the women themselves had not found energy to seek and courage to contend for it. What always chiefly militated against their progress was sexual subjection. The war against that has produced a long train of confessors and martyrs. It has been the chief inspiration of the poet Whitman, who crowns the line of native American Anarchists, and whose rapid increase in power and popularity is now manifest, aside from anyone's opinion about the quality of his art.

The dissemination of Anarchistic tendency has thus become sufficient to render ineffably ridiculous the plan of repressive legislation. Those who propose that, could hardly wish for statutes more drastic than were enacted in France after the death of Carnot. These laws, unequaled in cruelty and absurdity since those of Queen Elizabeth, and rigorously enforced so long as they could be, almost made it criminal to *think* Anarchism. They actually did make it criminal to defend Anarchism in conversation or private letter. The result is well known. Only eight years have passed since then, and already the whole literary world of Young France is Anarchist open-mouthed. Is not one such experiment enough?

The real strength of Anarchism is, however, not in count of heads but weight of brains. Nothing, obviously, can be a more absurd, or I venture to add, more hopelessly "played out" way of gammoning the multitude than to call Anarchism a movement of the ignorant class. It has always been eminently a movement of the literary and scientific class. Its obstacles always were simple ignorance and the "compound ignorance" of half-education. But these obstacles are much too far overcome for restoration. As long ago as the Homestead conflict, a very unfriendly critic (Charles Dudley Warner), while lamenting the growth of Anarchism among the masses, confessed that it "came down from serene heights." Like the Prophet who, for solitary converse with Jehovah, scaled the mountains on whose summit there is always sunshine, the Anarchist stands above the clouds and beholds the uproar and darkness pass away beneath his feet. The doctrine of Anarchism is the truth of Science. The power which secures the progres of Truth is omnipotence. No weapons framed against her shall prosper. Fulminations against what can be proved, are decrees against the earth's motion. Whatever they may hurt, they will not hurt the demonstration. They can neither prevent the earth from moving, nor even their promulgators from moving with the earth.